*Shades of Sorrow,
Tears & Laughter*

Shades of Sorrow, Tears & Laughter

Beatrice Fri Bime

Spears Books

Spears Books
An Imprint of Spears Media Press LLC
7830 W. Alameda Ave, Suite 103-247
Denver, CO 80226
United States of America

First Published in the United States of America in 2021 by Spears Books
www.spearsmedia.com
info@spearsmedia.com
@spearsbooks

Information on this title: www.spearsmedia.com/shades-of-sorrow-tears-and-laughter
© 2021 Beatrice Fri Bime
All rights reserved.

No part of this publication may be reproduced, distributed, or transmitted in any form or by any means, including photocopying, recording, or other electronic or mechanical methods, without the prior written permission of the publisher, except in the case of brief quotations embodied in critical reviews and certain other noncommercial uses permitted by copyright law. For permission requests, write to the publisher, addressed "Attention: Permissions Coordinator," at the address above.

ISBN: 9781942876854 (Paperback)
Also available in Kindle format

Cover photo: Vecteezy.com
Cover designed by DK
Designed and typeset by Spears Media Press LLC

Distributed globally by African Books Collective (ABC)
www.africanbookscollective.com

To Gladys Lumnwi Njong née Tanifum, for pushing me to and believing that I could.
I love you.

CONTENTS

Foreword   xi

Part 1
Poems of Reminiscence   xiii

If	1
What If?	3
Posthumous	4
My Heart Is Tearing	5
Green Tea	7
Douala-Yaounde	8
Reconnecting	10
Memories	11
Reflection	13
Yaounde en Fête	15
The Fear	17
A Moment in Time	19

Part 2
Poems of Optimism   21

We Can Shine	22
The Rendezvous	23
Still I Stand	25
Searching for my Best Self	27
In the Storm	29

Part 3
Poems of Negritude   31

    Being African   32
    Peace Within   34

Part 4
Poems of Lamentation   37

    Lament For My Land   38
    My Pain   40
    Nameless   42
    Death   45
    Remembering   47
    Our World   49
    Double Pain   51

Part 5
Poems of Existentialism   53

    The Tears   54
    The Anglophone   55
    Disharmony   57
    The Smell of Incense   59
    Regret   61
    Crossroads   63

Part 6
Poems of Social Satire   65

    Limbo   66
    The Palace Clown   68
    Stuck   70
    Women's Day   72
    Gift Horse   75
    Parasites   77
    Power   79
    A Strange Land   81
    Having   83

Lessons	85

Part 7
Poems of Love — 87

The Treasure Within	88
Not Enough	90
A Touch of Paradise	92
Marriage	94
Drained	96
This Moment	98

Part 8
Poems of Conscientization — 101

My Brother	102
Tinted Glasses	104
Would you Shed a Tear?	106

Part 9
Poems of Nature — 109

The Butterfly	110
The Road	112

Part 10
Poems of Oppression — 115

I Don't Understand	116
I Don't Like What I See	118
Beyond Madness	120
Orphaned	122
No Place to Hide	124
Empty	126
Missed the Point	128

Part 11
Poems of Gratitude 131

    Thankful 132
    My Friend 134
    The Most Important Thing 135

Part 12
Miscellaneous Poems 137

    Witnesses 138
    Lonely In a Crowd 140
    Farewell 141

Acknowledgements 143
About the Author 147

FOREWORD

Unlike Rastafarians who must distinguish themselves with crowding and clouding dreadlocks, poets must not necessarily make their outfit special in any way in their day-to-day lives in order to be identified as poets. You won't know that they are poets till they tell you, or someone tells you. You won't know that Beatrice Fri Bime is a poet. When you read her poems, you may not even know they are poems – but they are! Her lines are short, simple, straightforward, intelligible, and extremely rich in meaning and wisdom.

We have been carried away to think that poetry must be difficult to understand, that the language of poetry must be highly embellished, and that poetry must be overloaded with heavy metaphors, imagery and regular rhyme patterns. It took fifty years of criticisms and counter-criticisms for William Wordsworth's free verse poetry to be formally recognised by the British Society of Poets. Beatrice Fri Bime's style is in the tradition of John Donne, the most popular of the Metaphysical Poets. Like Donne, her love poems are pregnant with witty, but sober phrases and syllogisms. All her poems are short, precise, captivating and discerning. In the most part, they flow freely. She invests more in her subject matter than in her style – although her style is equally peculiar. Hardly has any Cameroonian poet of English Language expression succeeded in this poetic sobriety as she has succeeded. A typical example of this characteristic is found in the citation below from her poem titled "Farewell":

When the song plays and
I cannot sing the chorus,
Then know,
I would have gone to sing it on the other side.

When the dawn breaks and
I'm not there to see it with you,
I would have gone where there is no darkness.

She possesses in abundance, that argumentative shrewdness of John Donne in his poem titled "The Flea" in which he writes:
Live three lives in one flea spare.

In her poem titled "Lessons", Beatrice baffles her readers with the complexity of humanity when she says:
I have learnt, too late maybe,
That people don't mean what they say
Or say what they mean.
I have learnt that I still have a lot to learn.

Beatrice Fri Bime's poetry also resembles that of a Kenyan poet, Jared Angira. When you read most of her poems of reminiscence, especially those set between Victoria, Douala and Yaounde, you are tempted to think that you are reading Angira's poem titled "A Look in the Past". Her themes are centred around societal vices and virtues, human behaviour, pain, regret, greed, bigotry, and their consequences. She is a modern metaphysical poet comparable to the Italian statue, Janus, who has one side of his face in laughter while the other cries. As you read her poetry, you won't really laugh, neither will you really cry. Yet, you would personally confess having graduated from a literary college of incisive wisdom. You won't take her fervent believe in God as the infinite solution to every human problem on earth for granted.

This is her first collection of sixty-six poems to be published. Some of her poems have already been adopted for use by the higher educational curriculum of Cameroon, and this one has the potential to be used in higher educational institutions beyond Cameroon. It will prepare the minds of the students of this level to start looking at the human person, nature and life from a critical perspective which will strengthen their philosophical faculty, especially those who would further engage the Humanities and Modern Letters. It will tune them on to start asking themselves whether what they admire is worth admiring, and whether what they condemn should be condemned.

Nkwetatang Sampson

1
Poems of Reminiscence

If

If I could hold on to yesterday.
I will have a rose in my arms
And a smile on my face.
I will feel your soft palms in mine,
And your cool and gentle lips on mine.

If I could hold on to yesterday.
There will be laughter at the dinner table,
As I stare at the twinkle in your eyes,
And the smile on your face.

If I could hold on to yesterday.
I will watch you pour the Champagne,
And then pause and ask if I want,
To make it a kirroyale.
I will tingle as you pass me the glass
And make a toast to us.

If I could hold on to yesterday
My head will be on your laps as
You silently play with my hair
And smell the perfume of my body.

If I could hold on to yesterday.
I will hold on to you tightly.
And never let you walk away from me.

If I could hold on to yesterday
I will show you how much you mean to me.
I will tell you with gentle whispers
All the ways you make me happy.

If I could hold on to yesterday
You will be sitting here with me.
If I could hold on to yesterday

I won't be here now.

All I have is now
All I know is me
You were a part of me
That went with yesterday.

If

What If?

Like two ships slowly sailing on the blue sea
They brushed by each other
A second, that flight second,
They recognised each other.
The moment passed as each went their different ways.

A moment in time
Engraved on their hearts,
In their eyes and on their minds

A moment lost
A love found
A moment in time
A second

What if?
The moment had come
The second earlier or later
What if?

But the moment is gone
Gentle breeze caressing the waves
Two loves brushed by each other

They search,
Will they find each other?
What if?
What if?

Posthumous

He died to hear them
Words so strong, so beautiful
The words he died to hear,
Falling on ears so cold
The words he died to hear.

He lay in his new blue suit
The collar of the white new shirt,
Spread across the neck of the jacket,
A black bow tie tied round the shirt
Listening to the words he died to hear.

Huge candles stood on gold chandeliers
Providing the light to the path he died to see.
The perfume he died to smell
Came from flowers fresh and artificial
Cascades and cascades of them
The flowers he died to smell.

He lay on a bed soft and feathery
With sheets white as snow
Silky to the feel
The silk he died to feel.

The pillow was hard but smooth
The small pillow
Large enough to support his head,
The head he had died to be supported.

He looked at the large crowd
The crowd that came from everywhere
The crowd he had died for them to cheer him.
He saw the tears
The tears he had died for them to shed
And wondered and thought
"All I needed was a rose".

My Heart Is Tearing

It is scattering in all directions
The pieces are everywhere
Oh, my heart,
Why does it hurt so much?
Because you,
Who shared my bed
You,
Who shared my food
You,
Who drank my wine
You,
Who broke bread with me
You,
Who ate salt with me
You,
Who shared jokes with me
You,
Who sat at my table
You,
Who cried with me
You,
Who danced with me
You,
Who hoped with me
You,
Whose hand I held
You,
For whom I prayed
You,
Who was welcomed at any time
You,
Who looked into my eyes
You,
Who saw into my soul
You,
Could drum up such filth about me

You,
For whom I was ready to die
You,
How can my heart ever be the same?

Yaounde, October 2, 2020

Green Tea

I met a stranger in a crowd
A stranger who stood tall
Alone in the crowd
The stare was long
But I averted and lowered my eyes

I met the stranger in a crowd
Over the shouting and bustle
I heard his voice
A lone voice in the crowd

I met the stranger in a crowd
He nursed a bottle of water
Clear liquid water amidst the beer

I met the stranger in a crowded office
He drank a cup of sugarless liquid
"What's that?" I asked
"Green tea" he said
Our eyes held.

Today I drink sugarless green tea.

Douala-Yaounde

The cat asked Alice,
Where do you want to go?
Alice answered.
I don't know and the cat replied.
"Then it doesn't matter which road you take"

We left at six in the morning
Our destination was clear
Our road was certain
Or so we thought

We had to be in Yaounde by noon
The journey took five hours max
So we would have time to spare
Our meeting was at one
So noon would be okay

But that's because,
We didn't take into account
The traffic
Or the work
That was going on
Or the road that was cut off
By the truck

But we did
Or thought we did

We pulled out of the station
The bus drove for 2 miles
And stopped
The engine was running
There was nothing to worry about.

Then the drone of the engine continued
Still, we were standing

The cars stood
Bumper to bumper.
No cars were coming down
None were going up.

The rain was drizzling.
The weather was dark and damp
Still we stood
Nothing to worry about
Or so we thought.

An hour, then two, then three
We were still standing
The engine was running
Children slept
Woke up and cried

Four hours, then five then six
People started to worry
All meetings that day could not be met
No one knew what was happening

There were no cars going
There were none coming down
People started to ask questions
We were grumbling

The bus inched forward a metre
Then stopped, inched again
And stopped
Eight hours.

We had been standing on the same spot
The time it would have taken us
To Yaounde and back
It was a new record
Even for the road without a plan.

Returning from Douala, August 7, 2019

Reconnecting

The phone rang towards twilight,
The baritone voice said "hello"
And my heart skipped a bit.
"Hello" he said again
And I automatically answered.

It's been so long,
But the voice sounded like yesterday.
What could he want?
What now?
"Can I help you?" I asked

"That's not the way to talk to an old friend" he replied
"Old friend?" I asked
"I'm not so certain we are old friends"
"Really?" He asked "I thought we were always, friends."

Easy for him to say
I could feel the hurt
The resentment trying to take over and choke me
The nerve, the taunting in his voice
The smile I could feel on his face

The memories,
The bad, the good and the ugly
I held the phone and heard him ask
"Are you still there? Did I catch you at a bad time?"

Am not sure what I responded.
Then he said "I will like to see you if you don't mind"
"Really?" I asked
"I certainly mind"
Did I say that aloud?

Returning from Victoria, September 25, 2019

Memories

Victoria, I passed through today
The roads had changed
The houses had mushroomed
Gardens had changed its
Wooden houses for bricks.

The flowers that gave the garden its name were gone
The street was tarred but the road was still narrow.

Down beach was crowded
The fish market was built
There was a booming trade
But the smell of the fish and ocean stayed

Roasted fish and plantains
Yeah, the council had put some order,
The taste of fresh roasted fish
Mingled with sea breeze
The cool evening air

New town had exploded
Roads, markets, shops, churches,
Hotels, houses
A mixture of this and that.

I walked through the streets
I wanted to see the house,
I spent vacations in
The site where I first fell in love.

The place where I matured
The compound
Where we were all one family
The Nigerians
The South westerners
The North westerners

Just people
Children being children
As parents corrected and taught us
Where eating and playing,
Was okay.

A yesterday that
Seemed like forever

I walked up half mile
There were houses everywhere
Tall and short
Old and new mixed together

Oh yes
I have been looking for a Victoria
That's gone
Even its name went
With the wind.

Just memories
Just memories
That's what's left.

Reflection

A simple question
That led to
A profound reflection

The sit-down dinners
Candle lit tables
Set with the finest
China and cutlery.

The water and wine glasses
The champagne flutes
Oh yes and the choicest of wines.

Soft music in the background
Music that teased
The senses
Tantalized and relaxed the body

The meals were
More than three courses
Depending on whether
They were African,
Or European.

One thing was certain
Whatever you took
Was finger-licking good

There was always
A touch of
Finishing school
In every setting or cuisine.
The subtle touch
Of elegance
Was matchless

Hate her or like her
That you couldn't
Take away from her.

Hmmmmm.
That simple question
That set me reflecting
My sit-down dinners.

Had I stopped them?
Or she was no longer invited?

Yaounde, December 22, 2019

Yaounde en Fête

The announcement came over the radio at the 8 p.m. news, then on TV
Some people left the government
Some new ones entered
Some changed their portfolios
While others were maintained

The dancing, the calls, the tears started simultaneously
Phone lines were jammed
WhatsApp beeped non-stop
Gates flung open as well-wishers,
And the not so well-wishers,
Went from house to house.

Congratulations Mr. Le Ministre
Congratulations Mr. Le Ministre
You deserve it
God is good
At last!

Smiles pasted on tired faces
Kisses given to known and unknown
Hugs given to people whose faces could not be placed
Hugs given to people whose names were unknown

The hugs were warm, some were exuberant
Others teddy bear
All part of the reaction after the decree was read

Champagne flowed like water from a tap
Water was shared
Wine bottles opened
Sweet drinks littered tables,
And side stools

Half drinks left in glasses
Some barely sipped
As the owners left them in the euphoria,
To move to the next house
Where action was taking place

People came in
In groups.
In pairs and,
Individually.

Some came in as others were leaving
They greeted at the gate
"You were here before?"
"Yes, we have visited and are moving to the next venue"
"Okay, we were just there"
"Bye oh"

Smiles, jokes and laughter
There was no care in the world
The bubble was just blowing and going up and up

Everyone was in agreement
About everything to those who were appointed
Those who switched ministries
And those who were maintained

On the other side the tears were
Kept in check
In a somber atmosphere

Yaounde was en fête
Some gates stayed opened until morning
The tip of the iceberg
The beginning of the journey.

Yaounde, March 2, 2018

The Fear

They walked off the edge of the lake
The body of water nestling between the hills
They got back into the car
All marvelling at God's awesomeness.

The descent was smooth
She dozed and woke up
To shouts of
Jesus, Jesus!

The car somersaulted
Once, twice,
And rested on its side
Against the side of the hill

They were four in the back
The Mzee asked if everyone was okay
Yes, yes the chorus came from behind

As she looked outside
She noticed that
The villagers had gathered
Round the car
Trying to help.

Three fat women
Including her were lying on her son
She could see blood
But couldn't tell whose it was.

The young girl behind became hysterical
Shouting and calling for her mother
The woman next to my son asked,
Are you okay?
He answered yes.

The people outside were trying
To see how to get us out
I was praying silently
For them to hurry.
The way we were lying
If the accident didn't
Kill my son
Our weight could.

The girl went out first
Then the other woman
And I asked that my son go out next
He went out and I followed
As the villagers helped us to the ground

The blood was from Mzee
He had a huge gash on his palm
Someone gave him a shawl
To wrap round the palm.

The rest of us had minor bruises
We were taken to the nearest house
As the villagers took out our luggage
And carried Mzee to the Oku health centre.

We checked each other
Cleaned out the scrapes
And took pain killers just in case

It's been months,
No, years
But I still hold strongly,
To the steering wheel,
When I descend a hill.

A Moment in Time

The breath that takes away your breath
Sucks in your breath
Stops for a moment in time
Suspended in space
Set still in time

There was no air
Everything stood still
Just the two of us
The two of us
In time and space

Two hearts beating as one
Time standing still for us
Just you and I
A moment in time

Ours to use as we wanted
Ours to cherish as we liked
Footprints set in stone
Not set on sand

The waters swirling around us
Just you and me
A time capsule
No space for anything else
Just you and me

A moment to hold onto
A moment in time
Our time, just you and I
Where does this moment lead?
Two strangers
Recognising one another
Just the two of us
Two hearts beating as one

Yes
A moment in time
What do we do with it?

Yaounde, May 17, 2021

2
Poems of Optimism

We Can Shine

I am me
With you, there is us
Alone, I am a dot
With you we are dots

I can feel you pushing
My feet are slipping with your shoving
I can feel your elbows pushing
My side is bent with your shoving

There is a cliff to my side
I am afraid to fall to the side
But I can feel you pushing
The touch is ever so gentle, with your shoving

I can feel darkness in the daylight
You don't feel my pain, you can't see it
But it's there, the pain of your pushing
The pain of your shoving

If you look, you will see
You don't have to push
You don't have to shove
The space is there to your right

If you only look, you will see
We can shine together
You and I
We can shine, together.

The Rendezvous

We agreed on a meeting place
We gathered all that was needed
And was clear on our destiny

I stood there
Day in, day out
You were two doors, down from your stop
I could smell you
I could feel you
Yet I couldn't see you

You never came to the door
Never came
Even when I stepped away,
I left signs that I was there
And waiting.

The light has changed
Days have passed
I now see the green flashing light
I don't know where you are

At this point, it doesn't matter
Where you are
It only matters where I am.

I am at the corner
I can still smell you
I can still feel you
Yet I cannot see you

I have to move my feet
It doesn't matter where I go
For our paths will never cross again

I need to move my feet
Any day now
My feet will move

I won't allow too many green flashing lights to pass
Wherever I end
It will be my new destiny.

(From Sia)

Still I Stand

They gather together
They plan their venom
They concoct all the filth,
Their minds can hold.
Still, I stand.

They kill me in their heads
They kill me with their words
They kill me with their eyes
They kill me with their push
Still, I stand.

They dig holds for me
To fall in
Sometimes, I stumble
But still, I stand.

When I'm down
They smile and laugh
Then they celebrate
But then, I stand.

The garments of shame,
They plan for me,
They end up wearing
As I look on
Because,
Still, I stand.

They put full stops
Where God puts a comma
And are shocked
Because,
Still, I stand.

Their insults fall like water
On a duck's back
Their stories
Spread like wildfire.
Still, I stand.

They plot like Cain
They dispose like
Joseph's brothers
Still, I stand.

The audacity
Create you cannot
Mend you cannot
Fix you cannot
Straighten you cannot
Yet you gather and plan
Methods, schedules
Where, when and how.

They come at me one way
And scatter seven ways
The fire of the Holy Spirit
The Blood of Jesus
Covering me
Keeps me standing.

Still I stand
Still I stand
Still I stand.

Yaounde, March 13, 2020

Searching for my Best Self

Because I put myself above anyone else,
Doesn't mean I don't recognise you
Recognising you doesn't diminish me

Why do you think that I should become small
For you to become great?
Why do you need me to submit
Without understanding?

As tall and arrogant
As you think I am,
I am still searching for my best self
The self I aspire to be.

I don't compare myself to anyone else
I compare myself to the me I am looking for
The me I want to be
The me that puts a smile on my face
The me that criticizes me
The me I can be silly with
The me that laughs at my imperfections
The me that stands tall in spite of them
The me who loves me for me

The me that hopes for tomorrow
The me that glows within
The me that shares that glow
And lights a light for others

I have been searching for that best self
Not to put out there
For others to see
The me that I see

That's the me I am searching for
The me my Lord sees

The me that prepares for eternity
The me that I want to be
The me that only I can be
My best self.

The self I see in the mirror
The self I can look at, without flinching

The self I can come face to face with
And still like it
My best self
The self I am still searching
My best self.

Yaounde, May 10, 2021

In the Storm

The waves came at me.
The strength, enough to upturn,
The boat
But still I stood.

My feet were planted,
Firmly on solid ground.
My back was leaning,
On the stone that was rejected.

The waves receded
Angry, furious and gathered
Their forces multiplied
Nine times. But still I stood

The challenges come
As come, they must.
Some I can handle.
Others HE needs to do so.

So, they look and wonder
How could she be so strong?
They know the secret
Or refuse to know it

On my own
I cannot stand
But He who,
Made this creation.

On Him
I stand
His promises He keeps
To keep me under his mantle

His covenant He keeps
His words return fulfilled
His orders last for a lifetime
His ways are different,
From mine.

So, on the solid rock
I stand
When the storms come.

3
Poems of Negritude

Being African

Being African has nothing to do with the colour of my skin
It has nothing to do with the texture or colour of my eyes
Being African has nothing to do with how straight or kinky my hair is
Being African has nothing to do with the language I speak or the ones that I don't speak.

It has got nothing even with the continent I come from or where it is found on the world map
Being African starts with the music in my ears, the blood pulsating through my veins,
The uniqueness and shape of my body,
The smell of earth on rainy days,
The sound of animals far off,
The height of the trees and the lushness of the grass,
The brownness of the earth and the sands for miles on end,
The blue sea and the blue sky.

Being African is the greeting on the road from a total stranger;
The uncles and aunts who are not related to me;
The smile from a neighbour and the blessings from a toothless old woman;
The knock at the door at any time and the assurance that the door will be opened and I will be welcomed.

Being African is the laughter I hear from the villagers as they drink palm wine under the trees near thatched huts.
Being African is the smell of flowers that grow in the wild;
The fresh vegetables from the farm and the fowls that walk round the house.

The dawn that is signalled by the crow of the cock;
The whisper of the trees as the wind blows their leaves.
Being African is the heat, the joy of sharing and the bonds between us.
Being African is the culture I grew up with

Being African is the way of life I know and accept.

Peace Within

She said
He said
They said
Who cares?

I have learnt to close my ears
To close my mouth
To close my eyes
To block the smell

I have heard them say things
About me I don't know
A me that lives in their imagination
A me that's a stranger to me
A black me
To make them white

I thank God for the air I breathe
For the food on the table
The simple things of life
The joy in my heart

I thank God for the smell of fresh roses
I thank God for the strength to look away
I thank God for the ability to get up
To move on
And leave them staring
Their mouths agape.

I don't owe you an explanation
I owe myself, a debt of happiness
I owe me a relationship with my maker
So, you see
Spend your time
Talk all you can
Imagine all the filth

Your mind can contain
It doesn't change who
Or what I am.

Yaounde, Mont Febe Hotel, November 26, 2019

4
Poems of Lamentation

Lament For My Land

I cry for the pupil who knows that he has to give his lunch to the bus driver in order to get a good seat on the bus.
I cry for the pupil who needs to take a packet of sugar to school to get good marks.

I cry for the youth who has left secondary school and can speak neither the Queen's language nor Napoleon's.
I cry for the youth who wants to work but has no marketable skills.
I cry for the university graduate who writes "*concours*" after "*concours*" and never makes it through the "*orals*".

I cry for the graduate who goes around with torn jeans and a defeated look.
I cry for the graduate who ten years after leaving the university can no longer enter the public service because he is 33.
I cry for the graduate who has to change his age over and over but retires never having worked.

I cry for the graduate who sleeps forever because he could no longer move his feet.
I cry for the man who has to retire at 55 just when he became a master of his craft.
I cry for the man who has to compile papers to have his dues.
I cry for the man who paid for land which was sold to four other people.
I cry for the man who took years for his case to be heard in court.
I cry for the one who died before his verdict came out.
I cry for the woman who died in childbirth because there was no hospital or doctor in the village.

I cry for the baby who survived alone while the money meant for the hospital went into another's pocket.
I cry for the child who wants to go to school but can't because there is no school.
I cry for the woman in the village who has nothing to eat while the money that could have brought her water is used to settle political

issues.

I weep for the parliamentarian who swears to represent his people but ends up blackmailing the system to send him on missions he doesn't go.
I cry for my country, the land of milk and honey where some have too much and others nothing.
I cry for Africa because I don't know where to turn.

My Pain

I can see into your eyes
Down to your heart
Or is it your soul?

The pity is there
The question is there
The wish, the longing is there

I want to reach out, to touch you
To explain
For comfort
But I can't.

Just the tears
That slowly come
At the sides of my eyes
The inactivity
The inability
The amnesia
The weakness

Yes, I wish I could explain
Yes, I wish I could share
Yes, I wish I could let you in
Yes, I wish I could accept

But you don't know
The pain starts from my toes
Spreads through my back
Up somewhere
Where they become,
Like a thousand needles
Pricking me.

I want to shout
To cry out

But the pain
My pain has taken my voice
It has taken my mind
Robbed me of everything I was
Everything I wanted to be.

The pain has taken over everything
It controls everything

This pain, my pain
You want to share?
How can I let you?

On the way to Douala, April 22, 2019

Nameless

She was a stranger
She wandered to the city
Running from the bullets
She was a nobody
She didn't know anyone
None knew her

Then she met the bike rider
He rode with her
Through the streets,
Without a helmet
The breeze blew on her face
She was enthralled
She was excited.

He shared his room with her
She cleaned and cooked
The chores women do
They shared his bed
There was no protection
There was no promise
Just a roof and a meal

Then she missed her period
She had never heard about protection
She didn't want an abortion
The fights started
The rides stopped

Alone in the city
Away from the noise of the battle
She faced another kind of battle
As in the first there was no one
She stayed in her corner
Alone with her mentor
Afraid of the gift

A gift that was not wanted
A gift that had not been planned
Two children
A responsibility
Above them
There was no prenatal
The money wasn't there

But to the hospital they had to go
She was in pains
The pains too painful
For the cry to come out.

She was falling
The nurses caught her
Oh God!
The babies started to come out
Triplets, oh God!
One wasn't wanted, now three?

She had no time to react
Her body was exhausted
Her mind foggy
Could three children have come from such a tiny body?

The nurses rushed out
Asking for help
The media was awash
With the information
The response was swift.

People, money, baby clothes
They came in their numbers
She will be fine if she made it
The children were all fine
The blood was infused
And infused.

But she never made it
The girl who fled the guns

From the village
To the city
The girl whose name
We never knew
The children left orphaned
Another casualty of the war
That was raging in our country.

Garoua, October 23, 2019

Death

The obituaries became daily
They had moved to the city
It was safe for now

The woman came to register
Her children in school
There were no schools in the villages
The war had forced them close

The children had been out of school
For four years
So bundled them, she left the village
And came to the city

But then, before
She could settle
She had a malaise
And never woke up.

The children were
Left alone
In a city they hardly knew
The community rallied
And buried her at "Science".

Her body couldn't
Be taken home
There was no one to,
The risks were too high.
The home she had never thought,
She wouldn't return to.

Another internally displaced person,
Another casualty of the war,
The next day on the forum
There was another announcement

Another IDP had died
The "Science" cemetery
Was ready for another body
That belonged somewhere else.

Garoua, October 24, 2019

Remembering

Today I wore black
My heart was heavy
My feet numb
My eyes swollen
With unshed tears.

Too many questions
My head aches
Too many questions
No answers

I wore black today
For the people of Ngarbuh
The children who were
Still waiting to see the light of day
Those whose dreams were cut short.

The president who would never be
The doctor whose fingers will never be used
The musician whose voice will never be heard
The engineer whose art we will never see
The journalist whose voice will never come over the airwaves
Because it was smothered forever.

Today I also wore black for
The family whose story was erased
By a truck driver.
The little girl who was looking forward
To this world.
The little boy whose dreams were squashed.
The beautiful girl whose father went before her
The magistrate who will never sit at a bench.
I wore black today
For the family that was in shock
The questions that couldn't be answered
A community in a trance

Plans that had to be suspended
In a society in tatters.

Today I wore black
Yes, I wore black
Not to a funeral
But to funerals
Remembering all of them.

Yaounde, February 21, 2020

Our World

I was tired, and sweaty
After hours of pain and pushing
The baby was placed on my chest, dew and all
We took one look at each other and fell in love

His shriek startled everyone in the ward
I smiled and something so magical
Filled my heart, my lungs and body.
His father walked in
The pride on his face made me forgive all his errs.

My son and I
We have been together, just him and I since he was four
The memories of a father faint, just a name and a face
But us, we have been there, each for the other.

The bond grew
With every word he uttered
With every sound he made
With every step he took
With every cry when he hurt
With every report card he brought.

We talked about everything and nothing
He talked about his few friends
He talked about his first love
He talked about his difficulties
He talked about his insecurities
He talked about his successes
And his failures.

I talked about my work
I discussed my cases with him
I discussed my fears with him
I discussed my dreams with him
I discussed God, Jesus and Heaven with him

We talked about everything and nothing.

Yes,
We were sufficient with each other
My son, my love, my friend, my brother…

How do I continue this journey alone?
The test is a difficult one
I always thought you will say farewell to me
Not I to you
Now I have to prove all the lessons I taught you.

The sand melted below me
The rock got pulled from down under
The carpet got pulled from yonder
The earth dipped from under
The ground just became quick sand
The oxygen just snuffed out
The world, my world, just turned upside down.

Lord! Do I have the right to mourn?
Who am I to cling?
Who am I not to let go?
Lord! How do I look upon the cold face?
And know
That it's forever?

For Ma Justine (I feel your pain) - Yaounde, December 28, 2017

Double Pain

COVID death
It's worse than
An accident
It's unbelievable!

The family cannot
Bid farewell
The corpse is wrapped
In a body bag
The authorities have to be informed.

He becomes a statistic
Number 245 or something
No one can see him
He came alone
But the leaving is very lonely

There's no closure
You cannot hold his hand
Nor give him a bath
All the suits and shirts
All the ties and shoes
The gold cufflinks

They are meaningless
They have no value

The worst part is the stigma
You need hugs
But you cannot get them
Social or physical distancing
Prevents you from much needed comfort
Relatives and friend
They are afraid to come
They too, may be contaminated
Only the very brave or the closest

Dare to come
But even then
Social distance prevails

The pain of loss and physical distancing
Increases the barriers
My God, what kind of death?
What kind of burial?

Strangers you don't know
Take charge of your beloved corpse
They may even choose a casket for you.

There's no church service
No choir, no *aso ebi*
No food, no flowers
No booklets, no testimonials
No lavish entertainment
No wining and dining
No dances to celebrate
A deserving life.
Nothing.
Just nothing.
From dust unto dust.

And that hurts, even more
Than anything else
Death.
We feel your sting.

Yaounde, May 23, 2020

5
Poems of Existentialism

The Tears

They have no shame
They gather at the back of the eyes for no reason
Or a reason the brain cannot explain
And force their way to the surface.

The gentle drops
Shock and bring you to awareness
There's a reason for the tears
A reason you may not define
But a reason all the same.

The tears
They have no shame
They come even when and where they shouldn't
How I can control them?

The tears
They say they got their signals from within
What are the coordinates?
They just drip on their own.

The tears
They force me to go deep within
To search my soul
To search within my heart
To find the cause of the tears.

The tears
They drip, drip
Silently flowing down my cool cheeks
Forcing me to look inside
And force them to stop
Or let them flow.

The Anglophone

I speak the Queen's language
That's not why I'm Anglophone
I am from a certain part of the country
That's not why I'm Anglophone.

I am Anglophone
My mindset
My culture
My history
My outlook

I am Anglophone because:
I am a free spirit
Freedom to express my being
My surroundings
To ask questions
To participate, not to follow

I am an Anglophone
I have a world view
I participate in everything
I can ask questions
And make contributions

I am an Anglophone
My Spirit is free
It hates to be caged
If you cage me, I must fight.

I am an Anglophone
I have been taught
To serve, not to be served
I respect hierarchy
I demand respect too

I am an Anglophone
It's my way of life
Different from yours
It's not just the education I got
Or the language I speak

I am an Anglophone
It's a manner of doing things
It's a lifestyle
It's much more than the language
Or the place

I am an Anglophone.

Yaounde, November 21, 2019

Disharmony

Tik, Tok. Tik, Tok.
My Husband was dressed
And pacing outside the bedroom door
I could hear the clock ticking,
Tik, Tok. Tik, Tok.

I turned to the pile of clothes on the bed
When had they become a pile?
I must have tried over ten outfits,
None fitted, too tight, on the back,
Others, on the waist, on the butts.

The eyes see the food,
The mind says it wants to eat
The mouth savours the flavour,
The hand feeds it.

I'm not hungry,
Not really
But the food was there,
It tasted so delicious.

My tummy was complaining.
My hand kept dipping into the plate
My mouth chewed
As my eyes and brain urged it on.

My tummy in reverse
Sent the excess to
My butts
My waist
My arms
My back

Atkins, Keto, coffee diet, egg diet
Vegetable diet, cabbage soup diet,

Maple syrup diet, low carb diet
Too many to count.

My mind, my hand, my mouth and my stomach,
Need some harmony.
Don't they?

The Smell of Incense

The agreement was signed and sealed
The understanding clear and straight
Part payment to be done in diamonds
The agreement accepted

Except you refused to take the diamonds
Because incense smelled in the shop
And you didn't know why the incense
Or the reason for the incense.

I like the smell of freshness
I burn fragrant oils when I'm receiving
I think of you each time I light a match,
Under the oil.

I think of you as I smell the fragrance
No matter which
It takes over the lingering smell of food
It brings the garden into the house.

Then I think of you
And all the money you lost
Because of your suspicions
And misconceptions.

He was Indian.
So, the fragrance had to mean
Something else
So, what would you say my sister?

When you visit
And I have a vanilla fragrance
Or a rose fragrance
Or the midnight romance?

What would you say?
Will you go back and collect the dollars?
Or would you just let that
Huge balance go like the wind?

Because you smelled
A fragrance?

Yaounde, February 20, 2020

Regret

With pure joy He created man
In His image He created man
Giving him all authority
And power to suppress and conquer

In his freedom he first disobeyed his maker
In his arrogance he tried,
To build the tower of Babel.

His maker laughed at his
Foolishness and destroyed
The tower but forgave him.

Forgiveness is His nature
Because His essence is mercy
His love infinite.

But the more He forgave
And forgets, the more man's excesses.
Man redefined marriage
Man redefined sex

Man built weapons to
Destroy each other.
All types
Then man wanted to
Make man.

They replaced God with
Science and God still
Sat and watched.

How do you explain?
Giving everything and not
Receiving anything in return?

God watched man hurt Him
Time after time and His joy
Slowly diminished.

But He is a steadfast love
You say?
There comes a time when
Enough is not only enough
But too much.

Instead of destroying man
God watched them destroy
One another.

Turn back to me with
A humble and contrite heart
But would man?

Crossroads

He held my hands, his hand steady and strong
He looked straight into my eyes
And the words poured out deep from his soul.

"You are a very beautiful woman" he said
"I have never been fortunate to have a good partner,
One I could talk to and relate to,
One who could talk with me
I guess I never would
I am not a bad man, just a few beers too many though
I am a good man
I can separate the good from the bad and be helpful
I love this country
I love all people
I would help everyone."

Then he paused,
And left the rest unsaid
It was up to me to interpret.

I looked at him, at a loss to say anything.
This African American who loved my country and
My continent even more than I did.
He had one bad marriage behind him
But the scars were still raw and bleeding.

Then he got himself involved with a girl
Thirty something years his junior,
Before he knew it, he was trapped in another
marriage with three children.

She too was a very beautiful woman,
He was lucky to have her,
But I could understand him.
What does an educated man discuss
with a chick out of the night clubs?

Little education and nothing else
But he was in for the long haul.
What else could he do?
He stood at the crossroads of his life,
Stunned about the things he had done,
Those things he would have liked to have done,
Those he might have changed,
And wondered where all the time had gone.

6
Poems of Social Satire

Limbo

The cold seeped through
He worked up
The place was dark
There was no sound
He turned his stiff neck
Rubbed his hands on his eyes
To see better but the place
Was new.

Who was he?
How did he get there?
Where did he come from?
What had been his destination?

Faint memories surfaced
He looked at his dirty, soiled pants
And wondered again
He thought he had known
Where he came from
And where he was going
The plans and the education.

He had it all
Parents who provided for everything
Education in the best schools
Graduating the top of his class

The money
The girls and the parties
The woman he thought was
His happily ever after.
What a joke?
Then the drinking
And the partying
And more women

Now he found himself in a ditch
On a cold lonely road
Not remembering how he got there
But knowing he had to get up and move his body.

If he wanted to reach his destination
But what was the destination?
If only he could remember.

The Palace Clown

He danced up and down
He shouted, he spattered
Insults, accusations and venom
Nobody took him seriously.

He continued to dance
Up and down
His face changing
Just as clowns do

They laughed
They ignored him
They didn't think
He couldn't be bothered

He gathered a ragtag
They could join him
To dance, to shout.

To make noise,
He was just a nuisance,
They thought
The ragtag grew and grew.

Before they knew it
He was their party's nominee
They held their breath
What a joke!

The clown, the ragtag?
It was going to be easy
So, they thought.
Until they got up the next day
To see the clown on the palace seat
The world held its breath
Wondering if they were dreaming

The palace clown was on the palace stool.

Yaounde, October 15, 2020

Stuck

They beat their chests like the gorilla
They stood tall and strong
Because they were the best
The strongest

Then a little corny virus
Manufactured from the lab
Or sent by God
Sent them into hiding.

Airports are shut down
There is no school
For the children
No hospital big enough

The distance between them
Is longer than before
As we search for a cure
For this "corny virus".

Powerful and yet weak
Send American bombs to destroy Corona Virus
Send the best researchers
To find a cure
As the death toll rises.

They thought they were enough
They could do it on their own
On their own
Without God.

Give God His glory
We are nothing
We are stuck
A little virus has brought man to his knees.

If we repent.
Maybe God will hear and answer us humans
Where do precautions take us to?
Africa needs more prayers
Doubt God not believing,
Human supremacy
Let them now show it,
Human pride
Let's go on our knees.

Can science solve all these problems?
With God the impossible becomes possible.
We are nothing without God.
Be under God's guidance
In whom do I put my pride?

The woman at the fountain was
Looking for water.
The woman met the living water.
Jesus breaks all boundaries
Jesus is the spring of living water
Can we seek Jesus at this critical moment?

We live in houses built with high fences,
We isolate ourselves,
We don't know our neighbours,
We are independent.

Break the fences
Around our houses,
Which do not provide shelter
Open them for the homeless
Or those running from the rain
Wells of living water.

Yaounde, March 15, 2020

Women's Day

One day? Every day?
Women's rights
Women's equality
Women's emancipation
I salute all women
Everyday.

Especially today,
I celebrate my sisters,
Every day, especially today
I reflect about life,
My life, your life
My successes, your achievements.

I look at the balance sheet,
I truly should celebrate
But I want much more.
I want the right to simply be,
I want the space to excel
With you,
Holding each other's hand.

Leading and showing,
Sharing and learning,
Leaving the footsteps,
For you and you and you
To follow
To make it easier.

I don't like the fabric,
With the letters and symbols,
That don't express me.
I hate the scramble,
And the march pass,
The women who
Have stood under the sun

Waiting to show their styles,
Their energy, their what?

They troop pass
Thousands of them
Singing and dancing
Before their peers
Hmmm!

The parties afterwards
The bars all filled with women
Dancing and gyrating
All day, to the next day

The families starved
Because the woman had to cook
But went marching
Those who would be beaten
The following morning.

And those who would sleep
On the roadside.
Those who would not remember
The next day what happened.

The euphoria of this day
Today only,
Or every day?
I salute you my sister,
I celebrate you my sister
From the fringes.

This year, I cannot,
Even smile
My sister,
The other sister
She, you, me,
Her children, all
Cannot join us
Because they were silenced.

Please let me be,
Let me remember her,
You, me and she.

Yaounde, March 8, 2020

Gift Horse

The water splashed on the banks
He walked with head bent low
Trying hard to understand
How did he get here?

She was beautiful
She was intelligent
She could cook
His mouth watered
"She had no match in bed" he said.
She was all he had waited for all these years.

He had found her
He was dizzy with delight
He was scared,
She was an image
In his mind.

When he touched her
Felt her, smelled her
Then he knew the gods had smile
d on him
How had he become so lucky?

Her long limbs
Slim body, tiny waist
Oval face, pointed nose
And shimmering eyes
Were gifts wrapped in silk,
And tied with ribbons,
A gift from the gods.

She was a perfect gift the gods had given him,
How had he become so lucky?
Sometimes he was afraid to touch her,
He didn't want to find out if it was a dream.

Her soft touch,
Her bubbling laughter,
And gentle touch,
Told him she was real.

He sighed deeply,
He could always smell her perfume.
This nymph, this angel,
This woman he had searched for all his life.

How had he lost her?
He was standing there alone,
With a stranger in his house,
In his bed.
Because he had kicked a gift horse
In the mouth.

On the Bus to Douala, December 7, 2017

Parasites

They suck the blood
Out of the state
The state pours
Money into them,
Like one pouring
Water into a basket.

The parastatals,
Suck and suck,
And give nothing back.

The state keeps them,
The mother cow being milked.
They justify
Social service
A necessity.

They pay them huge salaries,
They go to work when they want,
They sit at their tables and
Chat on the phone.

They are children of,
They are wives of,
They are brothers of,
They are nieces of,
They are nephews of,
They are cousins of,

Most, square pegs in round holes
Why should they work?
They are children of,
They are wives of,
They are brothers of,
They are nieces of,
They are nephews of,

They are cousins of,

The handfuls of nobodies
Do the jobs of everybody.
Complain? How?
They are lucky to be there,
They are not;

Children of,
Wives of,
Brothers of
Nieces of,
Nephews of
Cousins of.

Douala, January 23, 2018

Power

It sucks you like quicksand,
The lure of the acolytes,
The simple things
That first they ask.
Easy to give up,
Easy to live without.

In exchange for the car today,
The house tomorrow,
The position now,
The promotion tomorrow,
The suits and the wine,
The women and the cash.

Then your parents,
They demand
You or them they say,
If you want to continue.
The taste of the lights,
The shouts of crowd.

You give and justify,
Then cry, and cry and cry,
You know what you have done
The tears, for them or for you?
But the choice,
It had to be made.

The nightmare starts,
The headaches,
The stomach aches,
The ulcers,
The shine that's not so shiny.

The alcohol and more alcohol
To numb the pain and the guilt,

Then they ask the next and the next,
It becomes easier and easier.

But the taste of the power,
Isn't as sweet as it looked
Because the price
Is those you wanted to share it with.

Power, power and power.

Yaounde, May 3, 2020

A Strange Land

A palace he built
In the village he built it,
Standing three floors high,
With shapes and angles,
Stones, concrete and marble,
The palace in the village.

He was to "cry" his mother there,
All his big friends,
With their big cars,
Had planned to be there.

The army was mobilised,
Security would be tight,
A gathering as such
Had never been seen
In the village.

Then the accident happened,
The royal burial for mom
Was forgotten,
As he fought for his life.

All plans cancelled,
Mamie was buried
Like a queen
But it was not royal.

Today his death was announced,
COVID-19 had claimed his life,
Now his body would
Be laid in a hastily dug grave.
No family or friends,
No large farewells
Alone on his journey
Of no return.

His family cannot mourn,
They too must be tested
They will have to be quarantined
Cut off from comfort
For 14 days.

The pain isn't just the death,
The pain in the exclusion,
The pain in the burial,
No ceremony, nothing

The palace in the village,
Stands waiting
For a far-off stranger
Lying in a strange land.

Yaounde, April 25, 2020

Having

He has many shoes,
Tons of clothes,
A fleet of cars
Tons and tons of…

Houses, land
Everywhere, every day
Too much to count
In the midst of…

Those without clothes
Those without shoes
Those without food
Those without a roof
Those without a tomorrow…

He sits in his glass tower
Smokes Cuban and Russian cigars
Drinks crystal champagne
Eats toast with caviar
Rides with an escort of twelve

Drinks the best wines
With imported cheese
Served with a variety
Fit only for a king
Burps when he finishes
And stretches to relax

The servants are there
To pamper to his every wish
He checks his Bank Statements
And smiles
A Cheshire smile
The account grows on the paper
It's shown on

This in the midst of
Those without clothes
Those without shoes
Those without food
Those without a roof
Those without tomorrow....

Having, having and having
What does it mean?

September 13, 2020

Lessons

She smiled with her lips,
She swerved with her hips,
She stood on her toes,
And worked the shoes.

She spoke with her mouth,
Her heart hid the venom in her laugh,
She parted with her hands,
Her palms hid the poison in her arms.

She stretched her arms for the embrace,
Her chest hid the spears in her bosom
Her lips pecked her cheeks
Her face covered the nausea in her throat

"Wow! Congratulations," she said,
Her eyes veiled the anger within,
Her mouth said you look beautiful,
Her lips covered the why her,

She said I love you,
Her heart covered the hate in it,
She said, I would do anything for you,
The words covered the plans she had,

It really doesn't matter,
But it really did matter,
And her mind was already
Planning the revenge.

I have learned, too late maybe
That people don't mean what they say
Or say what they mean
I have learned that I still have a lot to learn.

7
Poems of Love

The Treasure Within

I watched you walk toward me
But you stopped and sat down
Your head bowed, your shoulder stooped
Why did you stop?

My heart aches to see you like that
I want to run to you
But my legs won't carry me
I take a step and stop
Why did I stop?

I want to wrap my arms around you,
To let the warmth in my heart,
Heat your body and melt the cold
To take away any lingering pain
Would you let me?

I want to sit quietly by you
And offer my shoulder as a
Pillow for your head.
I want to sit quietly by you,
And let you be.

I want to give you me,
To share some of the shackles that
Keep you chained where you are.

I want to give you my ears,
So they can listen to the thing.
You can share with no one else,
My ears are here if you need them.

I want to look into your eyes,
So yours can see through to my heart,
And see not only the warmth but,
The love lurking there for you.

I want to open my heart so you,
You can feel the truth, nothing can hide,
The truth we both feel in our bones.

I take a step towards you,
You stand up and take one towards me,
We walk slowly towards each other,
You take my hand and look into
My eyes silently.

What do you see there?
Can you see past the threads?
To find the treasure within?

Not Enough

Their life was happy,
They were good together,
He paid the bills,
Worked hard to provide,
She kept the house clean,
Cooked his meals
And made home comfortable.

They laughed together
They joked together
Their life was good
Or so she thought.

The work became hectic
For both of them
He was leaving when she was coming
He forgot her birthday once
Then again.

He came in just when she was feeling lost
He bought her flowers
He paid her compliments
He made her doubt
He made her feel wanted
He made her feel desire

He was subtle but good
He made her dream
She thought of him
Compared them.

Then the magic happened
It wasn't planned
There was no thought
It just happened

She felt the fire from her toes to her head
Her body tingled

She couldn't stop thinking about him
She dreamed of his touch
Compared her husband to him
She couldn't say when it happened
But she looked at her husband differently

Her knight in shining armour was
No longer the same.
He was no longer enough.

Yaounde, January 2, 2019.

A Touch of Paradise

He carried her out of the car
Crossed the door,
Placed her on the couch,
Arranged her feet,
Held her hands as he smiled into her eyes.

She wanted to get up
But he said "Your feet are too dainty
To touch the floor"
"Oh, but I can" she said,
"I know you can" he said,
But I don't want you to.

He brought her food
On gold plates
And insisted on feeding her,
"It is my pleasure" he said.

He cooked dinner while she watched TV
He set the table
And served her
Because she was too dainty to do it.

He took off her clothes
He didn't want her to bother
Then put the bubbles
And placed her in the tub
She picked up the soap

He said no
Be still
Tonight, I bathe you,
Because I don't want you to do anything.
"Can I brush my teeth myself?"
"That I can also do for you."

He was gentle in everything,
He woke her with breakfast,
In china cups
He poured it himself.
Slowly and gently,
He fed her.

"Wow!" She exclaimed,
"What do I owe to that?"
He licked the sides of her mouth,
Smiled ever so slowly,
And said,
"Just a touch of heaven
For my Princess
Did you like it?"

Did she or did she like it?

Yaounde, March 2, 2020 (Elizabeth Mofor)

Marriage

The guests were gathered,
They came timidly,
They were as late
As the couple.

Looks like everyone assumed
It would start late
As most weddings do in Cameroon.

The groom and his men
Took their time,
It didn't matter
That they were late.
It was their day
And they wanted their time.

Then the bride and her maids
Danced in majestically,
They had to show the styles
They had practiced.
All the moves and they just had to be so,
The ambiance,
The joy, the dancing,
The multiple entrances,
At the gala just had to be.

It didn't matter that
It was late,
Everything was late,
The pleasure and joy.
On the faces of the bridal train.

As they danced in
With different music,
Different styles,
Held the crowd spellbound,

The time was forgotten as
Everyone watched and enjoyed the music and the movements.

Drained

You look at me
With expectant eyes,
A question on your lips,
Your head tilted back,
Your eyes deep and penetrating.

I stood by you,
I gave you my hand,
I gave you my heart,
I gave you my shoulders,
I gave you myself.

All that I had,
All that I am
But my hand slipped.
You pushed me away,
Your eyes wandered,
Your feet followed your eyes.

I was left standing,
I was left wondering,
I was left shivering,
I was left to find my way.

Now I'm standing here,
On the path I have forged,
Trodden alone,
Made my way mine.

You burnt your fingers,
You hit your toes,
You found the shine,
Not deep enough,
The grip not firm enough,
The journey not smooth enough.

Now you stand here,
With expectant eyes,
Questions on your lips.
Your head tilted back,
Your gaze penetrating,
Your breathe held in.

What answer can I give you?

Yaounde, August 7, 2019

This Moment

This moment
This place
This minute
This music
You in my arms
Feeling your heartbeat
Next to mine
That's all that matters
You here with me
My time, our time
All we have for now
Just you and me
On an island together
This moment
That's all we may have
It's fleeting
This time
No thoughts
No phones
Nothing
Just you and me
Our moment
This moment
Savour the taste
Of this place
The aura of this moment
The fit of two hearts
Beating as one
The correctness
Of this moment
You and me
Here together
My moment, our moment
You and I
This moment
To keep

To cherish
To hold
To remember
This moment.

Yaounde, September 24, 2020

8
Poems of Conscientization

My Brother

I thought you were my brother,
We went to the same school,
We went to the same church,
We both sang in the choir.

We ate together,
We played together,
We laughed together,
We farmed together,
Then we graduated and separated.

You to the army
I to university
When we met, we laughed
We joked together
You and I.

We cried together,
You and I brother.
Then brother, why did you lead them,
To our house,
Why our house, brother?

You watched them spray the petrol,
You watched them light the fire,
You watched them burn our house.

Did you forget Yaa?
She was in that house,
The house you let your folks set ablaze.

Did you forget Yaa's hot fufu?
On those cold rainy days after school?
Why brother?
I thought you were my brother.

Did you laugh?
Was there joy in your heart?
Were your steps lighter?
How could you forget?
How did we sit on opposite sides of a war
We had nothing to do with?

How did your mind get so foggy brother?
Why our house?
The same house you took shelter in?
The same fingers that comforted you?

I look at you and see a stranger,
Where did my brother go to?
What happened to my brother?
As I cry Yaa alone, I wonder.
How did I lose my brother in a war that had nothing to do with us?

It will end someday,
This war,
Whether we like it or not,
So, what will happen?
You and I brother.
Where will we patch the pieces?
How do we look at each other?
How do we share the same space?

Shall we meet and pass?
You and I,
Or shall we meet and shake hands?
How do I look at you brother?
I try brother,
The harder I try,
The more my head aches,
I don't understand,
Yes brother, I don't.

Yaounde, November 17, 2018

Tinted Glasses

The people expressed their wishes,
He heard them or said he did,
Then went ahead and did what he thought
They needed or wanted.

The people looked at each other,
Looked at him
And walked off,
Leaving him standing with
The wishes he thought they wanted.

He watched them walking
Away from him.
The bile rose in his stomach,
He foamed at the mouth,
How dare them?

The little child said,
"They dared because you don't see them"
"The dared because you don't hear them"
"They dared because you don't understand them"
"They dared because they are tired"
"They dared because they had to"

The man turned, he was alone,
Where is the child?
I have the guns,
I have the army,
I have the money,
What can they do?

"There you go again"
"You are not hearing them"
"You cannot feel their pain"
"You cannot feel their anger"
"You do not see them"

"How can you talk with them?"

Talk?
Who wants to talk?
With whom?
I will show them,
I will beat them,
I will lock them,

The little child giggled,
"What would it change?"
"The people don't care"
"If you take off your tinted glasses,
Withdraw your army,
And your guns,
Just maybe, maybe you will learn how to govern"

The man's hands were sweating,
His chest was pounding,
His breathing was rapid,
His clothes soaked with sweat.

It was just a dream,
Wasn't it?

Would you Shed a Tear?

If I die, would you shed a tear?
Would the tear flow freely?
Or you would hide it behind dark glasses?

If you shed a tear?
Would it be for me or for you?
Would you remember the laughter we shared?
Or the pain and the hurt?

Would you come to bid me farewell?
If you would, where would you sit?
At the front?
In the back?
Or at the side?

What would you wear?
Would you wear black?
Would you wear white?
What would you be thinking about?

Would you bring a flower for me?
What would it be?

A Rose?
If a rose, what colour?
Red, white, pink or yellow?
Would you throw it on the casket?
Or it would wither in your hands?
Would the thorns prick you and draw blood?

Would you bring me carnations?
If so,
Would they be red, white, cream, yellow or pink?
Would you bring me natural or artificial flowers?
If I die, would you remember me?

What would you remember about me?

Yaounde, February 8, 2021

9

Poems of Nature

The Butterfly

She comes in many colours,
The Butterfly,
She flaunts her delicate feathers
She perches where she wants,
Flirts wherever she passes,
Leaves broken hearts in her wake.

Pretty to look at,
Delicate to touch,
Easy to love,
Hard to catch,
Difficult to hold.

She flaunts her many colours,
Her delicious beauty,
Dances her way into the
Arms of one lover
After another,
Flirts with them all.

And quickly moves on when she tires,
Leaving her lover gazing after her
Longing for her,
But knowing she has moved on.

The butterfly,
Difficult to catch,
Hard to hold,
She lives her very nature,
Leaving broken hearts in her trail.

Smiling her way into the next venture,
Always seeking,
Always looking,
Never staying long enough,

Hurting those she touches
As she moves on,

The butterfly
Who can really hold it down
Without breaking it?

Yaounde, December 31, 2018

The Road

It snakes through valleys, mountains and rivers,
It snakes through forests and thickets,
Alone, used and misused,
Angry and aloft,

> Tyres skid
> Iron clashes upon iron
> Blood flows
> People groan

The road looks on with quiet indifference,
"You made me" it seems to say to us,
"You use me and misuse me"
"You don't seem to care"

> Trees you fell
> Mountains you level
> Rivers you change their course
> Or build over it
> Yet!

The forest looks on with quiet resignation,
It watches as its cut and cut,
Its hairline ever residing,
Its thickness thinning,

> Connecting villages
> Connecting towns
> On to cities
> Meandering its way through.

Some their journey begins here,
Others end theirs here,
I'm the start, the halfway,
And the end,

Depending on where you are,

> How many people pass over me?
> Hundreds, thousands, millions?
> It doesn't matter
> I start from somewhere
> And lead to somewhere
> Wherever your destination leads
> Wherever your destination begins
>
> I am the passage
> I lead, I strut
> I conquer, I point
> I am the road.

On the Bus to Yaounde, March 1, 2018

10
Poems of Oppression

I Don't Understand

He pushed me to the ground
Placed his boots on my neck
Asked me to ask my question again
How could I talk?

I could not turn my head
The ringing in my ears was loud
My mouth was swelling fast
He pushed me further into mud
And said, ask your question again.

I made signs with my arms,
Flaying them about,
He would understand that
I needed to get up,
But that infuriated him.

The butt of his gun connected with my jaws,
The pain was worse than the ringing in my ears,
I lost consciousness
The water woke me.

I was drenched to my pants,
The water entered my chest through my nostrils,
I was choking,
My chest hurt from coughing,
My eyes stung from the dirty water,

My clothes clung to my body,
Cold seeped in,
I was shivering,
Feeling pain all over.
I rolled with my legs tucked under,
I would kill for my mother,
I needed warmth,
I needed her soothing arms around me,

My mother,
God, what would she say?
What would she do?
The pain was unbearable,
I moaned and felt a slap to my face.

I was screaming inside,
The anger was boiling within,
I wanted to shout,
I could not.
The strength wasn't there,
I felt hands lift me up
And dump me
In the back of a truck,
I woke to a dark smelling cell.

The cell was crowded,
I was on the floor,
The others leaned over me,
There was a cacophony of noise,
My head was splitting inside.

I succumbed to the land of lalala.
I woke up as more students
Were pushed into the already
Crowded cell.

Their juggling for space
Pushed into my ribs,
And I screamed.
"Shut up" someone said.
"Are you the only one who was beaten?" another asked
We all had a purpose that morning
It was supposed to be a peaceful march.
How did it turn bloody?
Or why did it turn bloody?

I don't understand!

Yaounde, April 18, 2018

I Don't Like What I See

Men are running
Women are crying
Children are shrieking
There is confusion everywhere

The noise is deafening
Houses are blazing
Men are shouting
Women are crying
Children are shrieking
There is confusion everywhere

Boom Boom Boom Boom,
Bang Bang Bang Bang,
Oh God,
Where's my son, where's my husband?
Men are running,
Women are crying,
Children are shrieking,
There is confusion everywhere,

The heat of the fire is burning,
The smoke is blinding,
The smell is suffocating,
Men are running,
Women are crying,
Children are shrieking,
There is confusion everywhere.

The smell of burning hair,
The smell of human flesh,
The smell of human blood,
The smell of gun powder,
The smell is suffocating.
Men are running,
Women are crying,

Children are shrieking,
There is confusion everywhere,

The sound of running feet,
The sound of boots,
The sound of shoes,
The bark of dogs,
The mooing of cows,
The grunting of pigs,
Men are running,
Women are crying,
Children are shrieking,
There is confusion everywhere.

Clang, Clang, Clang,
Cluck, Cluck, Cluck,
Machetes against machetes,
Steel against steel,
Men are running,
Women are crying,
Children are shrieking,
There is confusion everywhere,

Men wearing pants,
Women naked,
Women pulling naked children,
Naked women holding wrappers,
Men are running,
Women are crying,
Children are shrieking,
There is confusion everywhere,

Oh God,
I don't like what I see,
When I close my eyes.

Douala, January 23, 2018

Beyond Madness

Man is supposed to be above other animals
Man can think because man is a human being
Humankind has not been kind to its kind,
The words came out slowly,
Sent to hell,
Neutralised,
Back to his maker,
Six feet deep.

They bragged about the number of people they killed,
They spoke about them as if they were talking about nothing,
Nothing of importance,
Nothing of significance,
Nothing of substance,
Nothing.

How did we get to such cruelty?
How did we get to skinning people as if we were skinning goats?
How did we get to burning children as if we were burning roaches?
How did we stand there and smell the pungent smell of the smoke
As if it was some sweet-smelling perfume?
How could we look on emotionless?
How could we rejoice in the death of another?

How could we, how could we?
Where did we hang our humanity?
Where did we bury our emotions?
Where did we cover our shame?
Where did we leave ourselves?

The pogrom happened,
One man's excesses
Mass hysteria,
Six million deaths,
A whole nation,

It would never happen again,
The world united,
Strong against genocide,
They claimed,
Social justice,
Hmmm!

Then Rwanda happened,
But it was so swift,
The world was in shock,
Again, they swore,
Never again, not under our watch.

But Cameroon happened,
Under our watch,
We looked on, perplexed.
Watching and waiting,
The killings continued,
Under our watch.

The numbers rose,
National sovereignty,
They argued,
Internal affairs, they said.

The blood flowed,
The killings continued,
Humanity became inhuman,
Worse than beast,
None with reason,

Yet all refused to see,
Or discuss the reason,
Another pogrom,
In our time,
Before our eyes.

Beyond madness.

Orphaned

I didn't choose my country
I didn't choose my parents
I didn't choose my colour
I wasn't given a choice.

I came to be
God's creature
In a country I called mine
With parents that were mine
Accepting my "kinky" hair
My brown eyes and dark skin.

I came without a language
I came naked and empty
Space to be filled by my environment
I learned the vernacular
I learned to speak English

Why am I "Anglo"?
Why am I "Biafra"?
Why am I «les enemis dans la maison»?
Is the house not "ours"?

I can understand your French.
I am forced to understand.
I can speak your French.
Why can't you understand my English
Or speak it?

You say I should go back
Where I came from
Can you show me the way?
Do you know where I came from?

I turn to find the way
But your guns block my way

I want to sing, to ease my anger
Your noise drowns my voice

Why do you treat me as second class?
Must I always assist you?
I can lead
Why don't you let me?

You step on my toes
Then ask me to apologise
Why should I?
You slap me and tell me to shut up.

How can I?
I wasn't taught to be quiet
I was taught to ask questions
I always need to understand

But you want me to keep quiet
To remain silent
If I do then I lose myself
I diminish me.

You stifle my murmurings
You lock my body
My mind keeps working
My mind imagines my freedom

The smile on my face irritates you
Your slap cannot take away the smile
You can imprison my body
But never my mind

I am a bird without a nest
A cow without a tail
A star without a perch
A lonely stranger along life's path
But I'm someone to the Creator.

Yaounde, August 25, 2019

No Place to Hide

The safest hiding place was the ceiling
Or so he thought
Then they started setting houses ablaze
And the ceiling became not the place to hide

He feared going outside
Afraid of a stray bullet
From the military
Or from the Amba boys
A bullet was a bullet.

It asked no questions
It left the gun and hit its target
Anything or anyone on its path
It did what it was supposed to do
No questions asked.

He stepped outside
Should he run or walk?
Which was safer?
The streets were deserted
The town was quiet.

But he knew unseen eyes watched him
The military or the Amba boys?
There was no way to know.

Which way should he go?
Right or left?
He was sweating and shivering
There were tears in his eyes.

Where did my town go to?
Where are my people?
How did we get here?

As he stood there
He felt the pain
As the bullet
Hit him in the chest.

Yaounde, November 18, 2018

Empty

I am cold
Numb
My eyes have seen
My head cannot fathom
My mind cannot process it
My heart is tied to my chest

The corpses
They were everywhere
Burnt chaff that look like
Roasted animals
Lying with burns
That look like burned animals

Valentine's Day
Hate, not love
For the women and children of Ngarbuh
Snuffed by the intruders

It was so sudden
So casual, it was surreal,
The men in uniform
Hungry or angry?

They drove in
To the excitement of the children
The air soon filled with
Sounds of gunshots,
Shouts of fear.

Running feet and shock
The houses lit
The houses on fire
Mute people
Acting without sound

Furious as they shot
People in the back
Shouts of people,
Burning in the houses.

The cries of the children
The shock of the villagers
Stupefied by what they
Didn't understand.

The bubbling village
Turned to silence
The silence of the grave
The fear of those
Who had managed to escape.

Yaounde, February 14, 2020

Missed the Point

Buea was the target
Trek, walk, fly
Buea was the dream
We accepted the fact
We will get there by all means.

Today you picked up
My brother, your brother,
Then you asked for ransom
As you tortured him.

Today a school was scorched
Children denied the same rights we had
A lot of things were burnt
All their beds, all their clothes
Burnt so they would stop going to school

Today children were shot
Eleven children
In front of their mates
The trauma, the pain
No one accepted
The cost of the collateral damage
The cost of the dream, the suffering.

The fight was not for a language
Another's language
No, the fight was for a culture
A way of thinking
A style of doing things
A way of managing,
Discrimination and marginalization,
Second classism, nepotism.

A call to stand and be counted
A call for more of the national cake

A call for doing things in a certain manner
A call to study in a certain style
A call for justice
A call for my basic rights
Human rights.

So, when you give out those other reasons,
You have missed the point.

Now instead of talking,
We are letting the guns talk for us.
Instead of walking, we are crying,
Instead of being under the shelter,
We are in the bushes.

You desecrated the values we held dear,
The respect we were longing for,
How could you enter our palaces?
Touched the untouchables,
And still say you are doing it for me?

Which me do you mean?
My sister that was butchered?
The six-month old baby that was killed?
The children that were slaughtered?
Or the families that fell together?

What about the houses that were burnt?
The old women who couldn't get out?
The babies that were charred?
And the schools that were burnt?
That dirt and chaff is all that remains.

You who say you're fighting for me,
You who say you're protecting me,
Both of you I don't trust
Because you have simply missed the point.

Yaounde, February 14, 2021

11
Poems of Gratitude

Thankful

The letter said
We would not be renewing your contract
The others looked at her
And couldn't understand
Why she was smiling.

She said,
"In everything give thanks to God"
I am thankful
For the opportunity
For the honour
For the lives I have touched
The changes I have made
The routes I have travelled
The people I have met
On those routes.

The opinions I have moulded
The lives I have touched
The lives that have touched mine
The lessons I have learned.

God might just
Be saying move on,
This was just a passage,
Not meant for you to tarry
Too long.

I don't wish to look back
But if I do all I remember
Is the joy
The laughter and the lessons.
The challenges
We overcame,
The way we grew
The way we fitted

Into the pot.

Yes, my feet
Are lighter as I look
Forward to a future,
Froth with opportunities.

Yes, I have no regrets
No tears to shed
I am thankful
For all the yesterdays
For all the tomorrows.

Yaounde, April 18, 2020

My Friend

I could feel your pain
It was there in your eyes
It was there in the way you stooped
It was there in your speech
It was there. Just there.
I wanted to reach out,
To touch your shoulders,
To put a smile on your face,
To wipe the tears off,
The tears you could barely hold.
You mustered courage
You will not let me see you break.
I could see alright,
So why don't you see that I see?
Your pain is slowly seeping into my heart,
Spreading into my body
Like cancer cells
It's spreading
Why don't you let me help you?
I'm stretching the olive branch,
Will you take it?

Yaounde, October 20, 2018

The Most Important Thing

Give me directions
I will find my way

If you give me money
I may not use it wisely
Send me to school
I will learn how to make money.

Hold my hand
I will stand on my own
Show me the way
I will follow the path.

Don't trace it for me
Rust may cover the marks
Give me directions
I will find my way.

Give me the advice
It may change
The direction
Of my life.

Pray for me
I may hear God speak
Teach me to pray
I will have visions.

Don't watch me fall
And laugh
Have my back
We will both
Stand tall.

Yaounde, June 29, 2020

12
Miscellaneous Poems

Witnesses

I alone escaped to tell you
The words Job heard over and over
Like a torrent of rain
The servants came
One after the other
No time for Job
To comprehend
No time to digest
No time to sink.

A deep ship
Couldn't sink lower
Job, you, me were
At rock bottom.
There couldn't be more,
Could they?
The farm he had toiled
The houses he had built
The children he birthed
The camels, the houses
All gone in a twinkle of the eye.
The judgement from
Friends, from his wife,
From his enemies
From his frenemies
The pain from the sores,
Too much for one man to bear.
The oxen and donkeys swept by the Sabaeans,
His servants killed by the sword
Fire burning all the sheep
Camels raided by the Chaldeans
Oh, that his sons and daughters were left out
But they too killed by a gale.
How stout a man was job
To take all this in
And praise the Lord

Who giveth and who taketh
Only witnesses to say what they witnessed.

Yaounde, October 7, 2020

Lonely In a Crowd

The drums beat
The music plays on
People swell all round me
Tapping their feet to the beat
Of the music.

I look for you
I see a head
Is that you?
I miss you.

Where are you?
I long for you to be here
Tapping your feet
To the beat of the music.

Talking with me
I want to share a joke
With you
Something only you will understand.

I look and look again
The ground swirls round me
Someone nudges me
I turn,
It's not you.

I want to share this
With you, you alone,
Will no one understand?

I'm standing in a crowd
Feeling lonely and alone.

Farewell

When the song plays and I don't get up
To dance
Then know that
I would have crossed to the other side.

When the song plays and
I cannot sing the chorus
Then know
I would have gone to sing it on the other side.

When the dawn breaks and
I'm not there to see it with you,
I would have gone where there is no darkness.

When the roses and the lilies bloom and
I'm not there to smell them with you,
Then I would have gone to the place where they stay in bloom.

When you call out to me and
Hear an echo instead of an answer,
Then I am gone to the place where I'll hear you always.

When you hurt or cry and
I am not there to wipe your tears or comfort you,
Then take heart,
I would have gone to that place
Where I will watch over you always.

When you wake up and
I'm not there,
Then listen to your heart.
I will be whispering beside you and
With your heart you can hear me always,
Because I will be there.

September 30, 2006

ACKNOWLEDGEMENTS

I guess something ignites us to write. I have loved reading and writing all my life and I write for pleasure. It never occurred to me to write poetry seriously until two things happened. I took a picture with Susan Apara at a German embassy celebration and a student at the Higher Teacher Training College (HTTC), Bambili saw that picture and was so elated that Susan knew me. Susan later forwarded the enthused words to me along with the photo. That was the first time I knew that one of my poems, "If" was being used at the university level.

Then I happened to be discussing my writings with my "younger sister", Gladys and wondered if I should publish a novel next and she said, "I think it's time to publish your poetry." Simple, right? Unlike a novel or things I had published before, writing enough poems to fill a book turned out to be the hardest thing that I have had to do. I am therefore happy to share with you these poems which have taken me a couple of years to write.

There are people in our lives who make life interesting and worth waking up daily for. To the following, I express my deepest gratitude:

Mrs. Grace Ngwe Ndikum, my other mother; for always being there all my life. For bathing each of my children after each birth; for quietly being a force behind who I am; stepping in and taking care of me when my mother died. I am grateful.

Mrs. Pauline Longla, for adopting me in secondary school and for remaining a constant in my life. I have not forgotten all the food you made for me in secondary school, during my wedding and always. I can never say thank you enough.

Mrs. Grace Pungong, for being my sister, my mother, and the voice of correction in my life.

Mami Esther Neh Fombon, for being my inspiration, for encouraging me, for showing me all the possibilities and for your Love. Reme, thank you.

Lord Justice Florence Rita Arrey, for all your love and care. Thank you.

Lord Justice Christiana Fomenky, my twin from another mother, my mirror, my conscience and my BFF.

Rita Ako Kisob, a lot wrapped in a beautiful package. My confidante, my adviser; thank you.

Agie Ndikum, my tips and truth person. Thank you for being there.

Electa Ngoran Tasha, my BFF, thank you for bringing me all the important people in my life.

Alice Ouedraogo, my boss, my sister from another country. Always there for me, thank you.

Elizabeth Mofor, a constant in my life. Thank you for always being there.

Frieda Kisob Banboye, my daughter, my friend, for giving new meaning to appreciation and loyalty.

For my wonderful children, Mary Sevidzem, Jenabu Abu, Synthia Jin and Chelsea Mbaku

For my sisters: Adela Ndi, Gwendoline Mbaku, Leatitia Andin Fombon, Bridget Nambouh, Vivian Ashu, Quinta Fombon, Florence Mbaku. Proud of the women you have turned out to be.

My children, Kerman Kifon Bime, Chiawa Litika Bime, Louisa Bungo, Kindzeka Akere Bime, for the pleasure of being your mother. I love you always.

I would like to thank Mr. Nkwetatang Sampson for taking the time to edit the poems and all the reviewers for taking the time to read the poems and give their blurbs. I am indebted to all of you.

I would like to thank my children and household for listening to the poems in their draft forms and providing valuable feedback.

Credit for the following poems, previously published elsewhere are in order:

A version of "Posthumous" was first published in *Tidepools: Peninsular college magazine* Vol 1, 1981. "If", "What If" and "Cross Roads" were first published in Songs for Tomorrow: Cameroon Poetry in English edited by Oscar C. Labang, Miraclaire Publishing; 1st edition (May 4, 2010); "Being African" and "Lament for my Country" were first published in Two Cents for Africa, Miraclaire Publishers, 2012; "Confusion Everywhere", "My Brother" and "No place to Hide" first appeared in *Bearing Witness: Poems from a land in Turmoil*, edited by Joyce Ashuntantang and Dibussi Tande, Spears Books, 2020.

I cannot end without a special "thank you" to the editorial team of Spears Media Press for their diligence in editing, their feedback and for making the work better. You are greatly appreciated.

ABOUT THE AUTHOR

Beatrice Fri Bime is the CEO/Founder of AKAABI GROUP Ltd, a global strategy consulting firm that delivers world class, customised solutions to business corporations, governments, international organisations and non-profit organisations. She is also the Executive Director of the JOSBI foundation, an organisation dedicated to providing educational opportunities to individuals in need. Beatrice started her career in 1986 working for the ministry of trade and industrial development in her home country Cameroon and rose to the position of chief of service before relocating to Tanzania with her family in 1997. She was until 2020, Project Manager at the Business Coalition for Good Governance (BCGG) in Cameroon. She has served as a consultant for various national and international organisations and was previously, Partnerships Officer for the Global Fund to fight HIV and AIDS, Malaria and Tuberculosis in Geneva, Switzerland. She was the Country Coordinator for the ILO/IPEC/WACAP project fighting against child labour.

Her poems have been published in magazines, anthologies, and edited volumes, most notably in *Bearing Witness: Poems from a Land in Turmoil* (2020). Her fictional works include *Mystique: A Collection of Lake Myths* (2004), *Someplace, Somewhere* (2005), and *Two Cents for Africa: A Call for a Mental Revolution* (2012). *Shades of Sorrow, Tears and Laughter* is her first poetry collection.

Beatrice holds an MBA from the University of Wisconsin Whitewater and a BSc from the University of Wisconsin Green Bay. She lives in Yaounde, Cameroon with her family.

ABOUT THE PUBLISHER

Spears Books is an independent publisher dedicated to providing innovative publication strategies with emphasis on African/Africana stories and perspectives. As a platform for alternative voices, we prioritize the accessibility and affordability of our titles in order to ensure that relevant and often marginal voices are represented at the global marketplace of ideas. Our titles – poetry, fiction, narrative nonfiction, memoirs, reference, travel writing, African languages, and young people's literature – aim to bring African worldviews closer to diverse readers. Our titles are distributed in paperback and electronic formats globally by African Books Collective.

Connect with Us: Go to www.spearsmedia.com to learn about exclusive previews and read excerpts of new books, find detailed information on our titles, authors, subject area books, and special discounts.

Subscribe to our Free Newsletter: Be amongst the first to hear about our newest publications, special discount offers, news about bestsellers, author interviews, coupons and more! Subscribe to our newsletter by visiting www.spearsmedia.com

Quantity Discounts: Spears Books are available at quantity discounts for orders of ten or more copies. Contact Spears Books at orders@spearsmedia.com.

Host a Reading Group: Learn more about how to host a reading group on our website at www.spearsmedia.com

www.ingramcontent.com/pod-product-compliance
Lightning Source LLC
Chambersburg PA
CBHW031321160426
43196CB00007B/617